So many of the gospel acc[...]

roles. A woman was chosen to carry the Messiah and bring Him to birth. The ministry of Jesus was not exclusively male. Jesus encountered many women in His public ministry. He didn't bypass women. He didn't minimalize their worth, needs, pain or admirable qualities. He conversed with, confronted, assured and comforted women. He healed, delivered, counseled and taught women. He admired, valued, corrected and looked out for women. He used women in parables, as object lessons and to deliver the great message that He had risen from the dead!

In this study we will look at a sample of the women Jesus involved Himself with. I hope and pray we will be greatly encouraged as to our Lord's great love and dealings with women specifically.

I hope and pray we would all be greatly touched by His ability to meet women right where they are. May we admire Him even more. May our confidence in His ability to meet us where we are, be strengthened as a result of this time in His Word.

Maureen Schaffer

Week One

The Woman Jesus Challenged
(John 4:1-42)

1. In John 4:3-4 we are told of Jesus' travel plans. What were they?_____

   _____

   _____

2. What does the woman ask Jesus in John 4:9?

   _____

   _____

   _____

3. What do we learn in John 4:9 about the way Jews saw Samaritans?_____

   _____

4. How does Jesus answer the woman in John 4:10?_____

   _____

   _____

5. Contrast what the woman was coming to get and what the Lord Jesus wanted to give her?

   _____

   _____

   _____

6. Describe this gal's past and present lifestyle.

_____

_____

_____

_____

_____

7. What thirst was Jesus seeking to quench in this woman?_____

_____

8. Look at Isaiah 41:17. What does He promise to do for those who are thirsty?_____

_____

_____

9. What questions did she challenge Jesus with?

_____

_____

_____

_____

_____

_____

_____

_____

_____

10. What are some statements Jesus made to her?_____

_____

_____

_____

_____

11. What did the disciples think when they saw Jesus talking to her?_____

_____

_____

12. How can Jesus' example of talking to this woman challenge us in the way we treat others?_____

_____

_____

13. Whose thirst was Jesus primarily concerned with?_____

14. What does this reveal about the Lord's concern for those looking for love?_____

_____

_____

_____

_____

15. If a woman has been sexually promiscuous, what hope does this story provide?

_____

_____

_____

_____

16. Read 1 Corinthians 6:11. Contrast it with 1 Corinthians 6:10. What does the Lord do to the sinner who puts their faith in Christ?

_____

_____

_____

17. What was the reason many from her town came out to hear Jesus for themselves?

_____

_____

_____

18. Her life impacted those around her. A changed life declares the true Savior. Does this challenge you to be bolder with the good news of Jesus Christ? Explain._____

_____

_____

_____

Week Two

The Woman Jesus Healed
(Luke 8:43-48)

1. Where was Jesus going when this woman came in contact with Him?_____

   _____

   _____

2. Describe what this woman was dealing with.

   _____

   _____

   _____

   _____

3. What had she done to be healed before this encounter with Jesus?_____

   _____

   _____

   _____

4. What were the consequences of those attempts? (See also Mark 5:26)_____

   _____

   _____

   _____

   _____

5. What did Jesus say in Luke 8:45 and why did the disciples think this was a strange question?

_____

_____

6. What did Jesus experience when this woman touched His clothes?_____

_____

7. What did the woman say to herself as recorded in Matt 9:21? _____

_____

_____

8. Why do some people only go to the Lord AFTER their own efforts fail?_____

_____

_____

_____

_____

9. How can we train ourselves to reach out to Jesus first?_____

_____

_____

_____

_____

_____

10. To what did Jesus attribute the woman's healing?_____

_____

11. What did this woman do to demonstrate her faith?_____

_____

12. How did she react when Jesus first asked about her?_____

_____

13. Why do you think she reacted this way?

_____

_____

14. How did Jesus speak to her when she showed her face?_____

_____

15. What "crowds" might stand between you and connecting with Jesus?_____

_____

_____

16. How can we press through "the crowds" and touch the Lord?_____

_____

_____

_____

Week Three
The Woman Jesus Corrected
(Luke 10:38-42)

1. Read Luke 10:38-42. Summarize._____

   _____

   _____

   _____

   _____

   _____

   _____

   _____

2. Who is credited with owning the house?

   _____

3. Contrast Mary's and Martha's attitudes and actions._____

   _____

   _____

   _____

   _____

   _____

   _____

   _____

   _____

4. Why did Martha think Jesus didn't care for her?_____

_____

_____

_____

5. How did Martha think Jesus should solve the problem? _____

_____

_____

_____

6. What did Jesus declare was Martha's true problem?_____

_____

_____

_____

7. What was the "one thing" Jesus guaranteed wouldn't be taken from Mary?

_____

_____

_____

8. How did Mary respond to her sister's confrontation?_____

_____

_____

9. What do we learn about Jesus' ability to defend when we are judged?

_____

_____

_____

_____

10. Have you been a Martha? Explain.

_____

_____

_____

_____

_____

11. What practical steps could you take to be more like Mary?_____

_____

_____

_____

_____

12. What step(s) will you take first?

_____

_____

_____

_____

Week Four

The Woman Jesus Warned
(Matt 20:20-23)

1. Read Matt 20:20.

    a. Who came to talk to Jesus?

    _____

    b. How did she approach Jesus?

    _____

    _____

    _____

    c. What does her approach reveal about her attitude towards Jesus?_____

    _____

    _____

    _____

    _____

2. Who spoke first in the dialogue between Jesus and this woman? What was said?_____

    _____

    _____

    _____

    _____

    _____

3. What could have been her motives in making this request?_____

_____

_____

4. Write Jesus' reply. _____

_____

_____

5. Given the way Jesus answers this woman, what can we learn about the way He sometimes answers us?_____

_____

_____

_____

_____

6. To whom does Jesus direct His question about their readiness to assume a higher position?

_____

_____

_____

7. How did they answer? _____

_____

_____

8. Have you ever thought you could handle a privilege only to find out the responsibilities that came with it were greater than you had anticipated? Explain._____

_____

_____

_____

_____

_____

_____

_____

9. What can we learn about the distinct roles of the Father and the Son in Matt 20:23?

_____

_____

_____

10. Did Jesus rebuke the mother for her request?

_____

_____

_____

11. How did He handle her prayer?

_____

_____

_____

12. Mothers often think they know what is best for their children. What does this interaction with Jesus teach mothers about praying for their children? _____

_____

_____

_____

_____

_____

13. Pause and pray for a greater trust in prayer. Ask the Lord to help you hear His response to your requests. Thank Him for knowing better than you do in all you might petition Him to do.

...You do not know what you ask...

(Matt 20:22)

Week Five

The Woman Jesus Rescued
(John 8:2-11)

1. What was Jesus doing in the temple? (John 8:1) _____

   _____

2. Who brought the woman caught in adultery to Jesus?_____

   _____

3. Read Leviticus 20:10. Who is to be put to death for adultery according to this law?

   _____

   _____

4. How carefully did they follow Moses' law, since only the woman was brought to Jesus?

   _____

   _____

   _____

5. What does John 8:6 tell us about the real reason they were bringing this woman to Jesus?_____

   _____

   _____

6. Why would people use scriptures to support an action when they have ulterior motives?

_____

_____

_____

7. What did Jesus do immediately after being asked what He would say?_____

_____

_____

8. What did Jesus eventually say after being asked over and over?_____

_____

_____

9. Whose sin did Jesus bring attention to?

_____

_____

10. Who was left with Jesus after the Pharisees and scribes departed?_____

_____

(John 8:11)

...Neither do I condemn you...

11. How has Jesus removed your accusers? Was there a particular verse? Did he give you courage to face them? Explain.

_____

_____

_____

_____

_____

_____

12. How did she answer the Lord when He asked her how many had condemned her?

_____

13. Read the following verses. Record your thoughts.
    a. Psalm 109:29_____

    _____

    _____

    b. Rev 12:10_____

    _____

    _____

14. What are Jesus' final words to her?

_____

_____

_____

Week Six

The Woman Jesus Helped
(Mark 7:24-30)

1. What did Jesus not want to happen when he entered this house?

   _____

   _____

2. What *did* happen? _____

   _____

   _____

   _____

3. Describe the woman who came to Jesus?

   _____

   _____

4. Was she coming to Jesus with a need in her own life? Explain. _____

   _____

   _____

5. Describe the concern a mother has for an afflicted child. _____

   _____

   _____

   _____

6. What does Isaiah 49:15 say about a mother's concern for her child?_____

_____

_____

_____

_____

7. What did she want Jesus to do for her child?

_____

_____

8. What did Jesus say to her?_____

_____

_____

9. How did the woman reply?_____

_____

_____

10. How did Jesus respond to her reply?

_____

_____

...she *kept* asking Him...

Mark 7:26

11. This woman dialogued with Jesus in a clear and deliberate manner. How can a woman keep a clear mind in prayer when she is concerned for someone she loves?_____

_____

_____

_____

_____

_____

_____

12. Describe what she found when she returned from meeting with Jesus._____

_____

_____

13. What lessons can be learned from this woman's interaction with Jesus?

_____

_____

_____

_____

_____

_____

_____

Week Seven

The Woman Jesus Commended

(Luke 7:36-50)

1. Who owned the house where Jesus was eating?_____

2. Describe the woman's actions.

   _____

   _____

   _____

   _____

   _____

   _____

3. How did the people of the city view this woman? _____

   _____

4. Record the thoughts of the homeowner.

   _____

   _____

   _____

   _____

   _____

   _____

5. Summarize the parable Jesus told the man.

_____

_____

_____

_____

_____

_____

_____

_____

_____

_____

6. What did Jesus ask him in Luke 7:42?

_____

_____

7. Record his answer to Jesus here.

_____

_____

> *...which of them will love him more...the one*
> *whom he forgave more.*
>
> (Luke 7:42-43)

8. How did Jesus compare the treatment he received from the woman with that he received from the homeowner? List the differences._____

_____

_____

_____

_____

_____

_____

9. To what did Jesus credit the woman's great love for Him?_____

_____

10. How can our sin try to keep us from drawing near to the Lord?_____

_____

_____

11. Why would great forgiveness produce great love?_____

_____

_____

_____

12. What does Jesus say to her in Luke 7:50?

_____

_____

13. Look up these verses on forgiveness and record your thoughts.

    a. Psalm 32:1_____

_____

_____

_____

    b. Isaiah 1:18_____

_____

_____

_____

    c. Micah 7:18-19_____

_____

_____

_____

> *...your sins are forgiven you for His name's sake.*
>
> (1 John 2:12)

Week Eight

The Woman Jesus Admired

(Luke 21:1-4)

1. Where is this story taking place?

   _____

2. What was Jesus observing?_____

   _____

   _____

3. What was this poor widow doing?

   _____

   _____

4. Who was he contrasting in Luke 21:3-4?

   _____

   _____

5. Did Jesus talk to this woman?_____

6. What do we learn about Jesus by the way He observed these people?

   _____

   _____

   _____

   _____

   _____

   _____

7. How do people measure whether someone has given more than another?

    _____

    _____

    _____

8. What did Jesus say the widow was giving out of?_____

    _____

9. How might she have felt about the amount she put into the treasury?

    _____

    _____

10. What would this woman have missed out on if she had dismissed her small amount and didn't bring it to the temple?

    _____

    _____

    _____

    _____

11. Do you ever compare what you have to offer the Lord with someone else's offering? Explain._____

    _____

    _____

12. How can Jesus' assessment of gifts—especially those deemed "small" by worldly standards— free us to give?_____

_____

_____

_____

_____

_____

_____

Week Nine

The Woman Jesus Defended

(John 12:1-8)

1. Read John 12:1-8.

    a. List the people involved in this story.

    _____

    _____

    _____

    _____

    _____

    b. What city are they in?

    _____

2. Look at John 11:53-57. Record what Jesus was facing at this time. _____

    _____

    _____

    _____

3. What was Martha doing?   _____

    _____

4. What was Lazarus doing?_____

    _____

5. What was Mary doing?_____

    _____

6. What was Judas' opinion of what Mary was doing?_____

_____

_____

7. What does John 12:6 reveal as the real reason Judas held this opinion? _____

_____

_____

8. How did Jesus respond to Judas' judgment regarding this woman's actions?

_____

_____

_____

9. What do we learn about the possibility of being misjudged when we do something for the Lord?_____

_____

_____

_____

10. How did Mary respond to the judgment?

_____

_____

11. How did Jesus come to Mary's defense?

_____

12. What do we learn about the Lord's ability to defend us when we are misjudged?

_____

_____

_____

13. What can we learn from Mary about how we should respond when we are misjudged?

_____

_____

_____

_____

_____

...Let her alone. Why do you trouble her? She has done a good work for Me.

(Mark 14:6)

Week Ten
The Woman Jesus Comforted
(John 11:18-44)

1. Read John 11:14. What happened to Lazarus? Who was Jesus planning to see?

   _____

   _____

   _____

2. Read John 11:17. How long had Lazarus been dead?_____

3. Where was Martha when Jesus met her? (John 11:20) _____

   _____

4. Where was Mary when Martha was talking to Him? _____

   _____

5. Describe the dialogue between Martha and Jesus in verse 20-27._____

   _____

   _____

   _____

   _____

   _____

6. Where was Mary going and where did the people think she was going?

_____

_____

7. In verse 33 we see Jesus was troubled. What was troubling Him?

_____

_____

8. Who did Jesus spend the most time with during this sad time?_____

_____

9. Have you ever felt like the Lord did not show up on time? Explain.

_____

_____

_____

_____

10. How can observing Jesus' care for Martha and Mary convince us of His great love and concern for us?_____

_____

_____

_____

_____

11. What are some scriptures that declare God's timing is truly always perfect?

_____

_____

_____

_____

_____

_____

12. How might we grieve with trust rather than with doubt? _____

_____

_____

_____

_____

13. Do you think either woman expected Jesus to raise Lazarus from the dead?_____

14. What are some truths you treasure from this account?_____

_____

_____

_____

_____

_____

_____

Week Eleven

The Women Jesus Assured

(Matt 28:1-9)

1. Who came to the tomb after the Sabbath? (Matt 28:1)_____

   _____

   _____

2. What were the women coming to the tomb to do according to Luke 24:1?

   _____

   _____

3. What did the angel say to the women in Matt 28:5?_____

   _____

   _____

4. Why would they be afraid?

   _____

   _____

   _____

5. What did the angel tell the women to do?

   _____

   _____

   _____

6. What two emotions did they have when they ran to tell the disciples?_____

_____

_____

7. Who met them on their way? What did He say to them?_____

_____

_____

_____

_____

8. Read John 20:11-18. What happened?

_____

_____

_____

_____

_____

_____

_____

_____

_____

_____

_____

_____

9. Who delivered the first message of the resurrected Christ, women or men?

_____

10. These women experienced weeping, fear and joy. How does Jesus address these emotions?

_____

_____

_____

_____

11. How can we take comfort from Jesus' encounters with these women?

_____

_____

_____

_____

_____

Date:_____

_____
_____
_____
_____
_____
_____
_____
_____
_____
_____
_____
_____
_____
_____
_____
_____
_____
_____
_____
_____
_____
_____
_____
_____

Date:_____

Date:_____

_____

_____

_____

_____

_____

_____

_____

_____

_____

_____

_____

_____

_____

_____

_____

_____

_____

_____

_____

_____

_____

_____

Date:_____

Date:_____

Date:_____

Date:_____

Date:_____

Date:_____

_____

_____

_____

_____

_____

_____

_____

_____

_____

_____

_____

_____

_____

_____

_____

_____

_____

_____

_____

_____

_____

_____

_____

_____

Date:_____

Date:_____

_____
_____
_____
_____
_____
_____
_____
_____
_____
_____
_____
_____
_____
_____
_____
_____
_____
_____
_____
_____
_____
_____
_____
_____

Date:_____

Date:_____

_____

_____

_____

_____

_____

_____

_____

_____

_____

_____

_____

_____

_____

_____

_____

_____

_____

_____

_____

_____

_____

_____

_____

Date:_____

Date:_____

_____
_____
_____
_____
_____
_____
_____
_____
_____
_____
_____
_____
_____
_____
_____
_____
_____
_____
_____
_____
_____
_____
_____

Date:_____

Date:_____

Date:_____

Date:_____

Date:_____

Date:_____

Maureen grew up in La Mirada, California with seven older brothers and no sisters. At the age of 16, while reading the bible, she was born again, NEVER to be the same. Growing up with an alcoholic mother, she learned to value the companionship and comfort of the Holy Spirit. Upon graduating from San Diego State University, she went on to become a Programmer Analyst. She has been a stay-at-home-mom, English teacher, and Zumba instructor.

She has four adult children who were home schooled, attended public schools and private schools. She is a grandmother as well. She plays guitar and ukulele.

She was diagnosed with a rare salivary gland cancer in September of 2012. She had a radical neck dissection, oral radiation and a gastric tube because she couldn't take anything by mouth for a few months. Adenoid Cystic Carcinoma is chemotherapy resistant. It is slow growing but relentless.

Radiation therapy has resulted in severe swallowing disorders and lockjaw so eating is quite the challenge for Maureen. In July of 2016 the cancer metastasized to her lungs. She had half of her right lung removed and part of her left lung. As of July 2018, multiple tumors have shown up in both lungs.

Her husband has been pastoring First Love Calvary Chapel in Whittier for over 30 years. Her children have gone through some major struggles in their teen/young adult years and she has seen the faithfulness of God through prayer, bringing them out and into a safe place with Christ.

She is the Women's Ministry Director at FLCC and teaches at conferences and retreats.

Made in the USA
San Bernardino, CA
05 February 2020

64019480R00039